Guide

Boost

Confidence

Strategies to Overcome Fear and Doubt So You Can Go Beyond Your Comfort Zone and Create a Powerful Sense of Confidence to Achieve All Your Goals and Create Your Dream Life

By Clark Darsey

© **Copyright 2019 - All rights reserved.**

The content contained within this book may not be reproduced, duplicated or transmitted without direct written permission from the author or the publisher.

Under no circumstances will any blame or legal responsibility be held against the publisher or author for any damages, reparation, or monetary loss due to the information contained within this book. Either directly or indirectly.

Legal Notice:

This book is copyright protected. This book is only for personal use. You cannot amend, distribute, sell, use, quote or paraphrase any part, or the content within this book, without the consent of the author or publisher.

Disclaimer Notice:

Please note the information contained within this document is for educational and entertainment purposes only. All effort has been executed to present accurate, up to date and reliable, complete information. No warranties of any kind are declared or implied. Readers acknowledge that the author is not engaging in the rendering of legal, financial, medical or professional advice. The content within this book has been derived from various sources. Please consult a licensed professional before attempting any techniques outlined in this book.

By reading this document, the reader agrees that under no

circumstances is the author responsible for any losses, direct or indirect, which are incurred as a result of the use of information contained within this document, including, but not limited to, —errors, omissions, or inaccuracies.

Contents

Introduction..8
Chapter 1: Foundations of Self-confidence......................................11
    Experiential Self-confidence...11
    Emotional Self-confidence...13
    Self-Esteem 15
Chapter 2: Why Confidence is so Important 19
    Dealing With Fear and Anxiety 19
    How to Be More Motivated..20
    Be More Resilient...21
    Work on Your Relationships 22
    Why Authenticity is so Powerful 24
Chapter 3: The Secret Code of Truly Confident Individuals 26
    They Know How to Control Their Mind 26
    They Have a Dream 28
    They Aren't Worried About What Other People Think About Them..29
Chapter 4: How to Start Developing Confidence.............................32
    Leave Your Comfort Zone 32
    Know that You Are Valuable...35
        Means Values...36
        Ends Values 36
    Accept Change 38
    Be in The Moment 40
Chapter 5: How to Stand up for Yourself...42

Know What You Want 42

Understand the Truth Behind Your Responses 43

Let go of Attachment 44

Put it on Paper Before You Do Anything 44

Create Some Time To Have A Talk 45

Know When to Stop Talking 45

Chapter 6: How to Keep Going After Failure 47

Accept Failure 47

Give Your People an Opportunity to Fail 48

Promptly Apologize When Necessary 48

Look at Your Failures 49

Carry On 49

How to Achieve Micro-Goals 50

  Put Them on Paper 50

  Specify the Goals 50

  Keep an Eye on Your Goals Routinely 51

  See Your Goals in Your Mind 51

Chapter 7: Actionable Tips & Exercises 53

Grow Your Knowledge 53

Appreciate Smaller Wins 54

Believe in Something 54

Cultivate A Firm Resolve 55

Work With Professionals 56

Visualize Your Confident Self 57

Believe That You Deserve Confidence 58

Chapter 8: Importance of Buddies 60

    They Want You to Be Successful 61
    They Are Good Models 61
    They Support The Growth 62
    They Make It Easier to Keep Going 62
    They Show Us the Power of Teamwork 63
Conclusion 64

Thank you for buying this book and I hope that you will find it useful. If you will want to share your thoughts on this book, you can do so by leaving a review on the Amazon page, it helps me out a lot.

Introduction

Have you been considering methods to improve your self-confidence? Do you sense that fear has taken control of a big part of your life and is holding you back from living your real purpose? Do you wish to ditch all that fear and have unshakeable self-confidence which is going to leave individuals in awe of you? Well, this guide is made just for you!

Nowadays, there are numerous people not living up to their complete potential because of the fear of failure, or what others are going to think of them. As a matter of fact, that is among the most typical regrets many folks have when they are close to their deathbed. Something which you need to comprehend is that fear is going to remove the sunlight in your life and leave you with a lot of darkness and unhappiness inside.

The bright side is that you could shake all that self-judgment and fear to make sure that you regain control of your life and live a deliberate and delighted life. The one method to accomplish this is to master the art of self-confidence. It is via genuine self-confidence that you lay a strong base for making better choices, constructing long-lasting relationships, and setting up yourself for success.

What Comes To Mind When You Think Of Self-confidence?

" Happiness is when what you think, what you say, and what you do are in harmony."-- Mahatma Gandhi

This is precisely what I believe acts as a formula for self-confidence. If you will live a satisfying life, then you need to have the self-confidence to pursue the important things which make you pleased. To put it simply, you need to show self-confidence in yourself; capabilities, character, and intelligence.

So, what is self-confidence? Well, the reality of strong self-confidence is living authentically. It is just about accepting your genuine self. To accomplish this, you need to trust that you have complete control of your life, and not allowing circumstances prevent you from pursuing your life purpose. You need to choose the value of your genuine self and never ever let yourself be defined by another person's opinion. The more you do this, the more it ends up being simple to express self-confidence.

When you grasp the art of accepting your genuine self, you are going to understand that the doors of possibility are all around you. You are going to be spoilt for options. When endless possibilities come your way, there is no more space for worry of scarcity. Quickly, you'll recognize that you can live an abundant life. This is precisely what I consider to be a successful path to unstoppable self-confidence and satisfying life.

Chapter 1: Foundations of Self-confidence

Experiential Self-confidence

When I was a teen, something which frightened me the most was talking up women, particularly strangers. Making the preliminary approach felt unattainable and made me feel like I had actually entirely lost strength in my feet. It just made me close down!

Now, 20 years later on, I can't wrap my head around what it is that I was so scared of.

The fact is, you and I could conquer fear and quickly do the important things that we once believed unattainable, just due to the fact that we now have experience. I had the ability to press through those frightening seconds and conversations. Now, I can strike up a discussion with everyone I discover, on the train, coffee shop, or at the workplace.

I have the self-confidence to do practically everything I put my mind to. It is much like learning to drive on the highway for the initial time. Initially, it was frightening, however, with time, you adapt, and your body finds out that it does not end you.

Well, this type of self-confidence is what is described as experiential self-confidence. It is the kind of self-confidence which you acquire via experience. You have actually established this kind of self-confidence at some time in your life. The initial step is to have the nerve to take risks and act. Every time you fall short, you develop that self-confidence due to the fact that you comprehend that failure doesn't last.

Something which you need to value are all the things that did not work out in your life since they enabled you to learn. It is thanks to prior failures that we have self-confidence nowadays. For that reason, if you wish to develop your experiential self-confidence, the initial thing which you have to ask yourself is what is the worst thing which may take place if you fall short? Are you going to die? If no, then there is no reason to pull back. You should comprehend that each time you act in opposition to fear, you increase your experiential self-confidence, and all the activities which are tough now are going to be simple in the future.

Emotional Self-confidence

This just describes the type of self-confidence which you are able to switch on at will. Well, here's an instance: I began working for a global company at the age of 22 as a project assistant. Once, for one reason or another, I wished to work from other city for 3 weeks. Nevertheless, I was so anxious to ask my manager for authorization to work there. Did I ultimately do it? Absolutely.

Well, I initially needed to prep myself psychologically. I began by brainstorming how I would stroll into his office, present my case, and how I would manage his answers. I produced a little decision tree with all the feasible if, why and how questions he would have and which my answers would be. This was to assist me to remain on top of my game so that absolutely nothing grabbed me off-guard. To put it simply, I required this to keep my composure.

What I was basically doing was using my emotional self-confidence by learning the suggestions and techniques for managing my body language to ensure that I do not send the incorrect message. If you manage your body, then you are going to have the ability to manage your emotions. On the contrary, if you fall short to manage your body, then your emotions are going to be going left and right.

What I just did was rehearse each statement I wanted to state, and how I would do it with a solid handshake, shoulders high and smiling face. What I recognized was, when you withstand the urge of crossing your arms and revealing your anxiety, the discussion streams naturally, and the other party eases into the conversation. That is how you acquire emotional self-confidence.

It is essential to keep in mind that emotional self-confidence serves a fantastic purpose, particularly when you are in a scenario that you currently expect; for example, a presentation, a tough conversation with your parents or superiors, a performance, and so on. Unlike experiential self-confidence, emotional self-confidence is not restricted to simply one domain.

The only issue, within this instance, is that having emotional self-confidence is not automatic. You need to delve into your inner self to switch it on.

However, then what do you do in such a tight spot when you simply do not feel like it? We are going to be diving much deeper into how you can stick up for yourself and different methods with which you can deal with hard circumstances that arise.

Self-Esteem

This is the inmost level of self-confidence and is the real description of unstoppable self-confidence! One misstep that individuals make nowadays is believing that self-confidence has all the things to do with survival. The hard reality is that there are a lot of individuals with substantial muscles, war vets, and even firemen who do not have confidence! They do not have the self-confidence to start a conversation with an unfamiliar person. You need to comprehend that self-confidence is a thing that, within this age and time, is broken by identity and not busted bones.

We frequently think: What if other people hate me? What if I hold the presentation and they neglect me? What would individuals think of me? These are all self-defeating concerns.

Having high self-esteem merely indicates that you have the supreme level of self-confidence due to the fact that in such a case, your identity is not shattered. Rather, your identity is self-generated. You should never ever allow others to form your purpose and identity. You have the power and the resolve to maintain your inner code.

The initial thing to winning high self-esteem is making sure that your genuine identity is connected to your standards and values. It begins by you recognizing and accepting that the only individual that is going to break your identity is yourself!

The second you stop believing that your identity is at stake is when you are genuinely confident. In case you measure up to your standards, there is no rejection, weirdness, or public embarrassment that can disturb you. So what are the actions which we have to take so as to live with peerless self-confidence and high standards? A few of these involve you attempting your finest, completely expressing yourself, being responsible for your joy, and constantly aiming to do what is appropriate instead of taking the easy way out.

What others believe does not matter. When you live by this mantra, you are never ever going to be at the grace of other's opinions. Allow your purpose to constantly be the leading light and do your finest constantly. Do not hesitate to do the important things that frighten you and give it your all! There is no chance to lose with such a mindset. Actually, you are going to acquire more than you might ever envision.

There's a phrase that goes: familiarity breeds comfort. For that reason, guarantee that you are subjecting yourself to circumstances which provide you a feeling of familiarity in case you are going to go to a meeting, scope through the program of the meeting in your head. In case you will deliver a presentation, go through it in your mind.

In addition, it is vital that you take control of your feelings. Take at least 3 minutes and speak up, while smiling and taking deep and slow breaths into your stomach to successfully snap out that tension, anxiety, or pattern. In case you make this your identity, you are going to discover that no failure, rejection, or embarrassment is going to shake your genuine identity.

Chapter 2: Why Confidence is so Important

Dealing With Fear and Anxiety

Utmost enemy of development is fear. Nevertheless, something that you need to comprehend is that developing your self-confidence plays an extremely considerable role in providing a relaxing effect. It merely silences the voice within you that attempts to encourage you that you can not do it. It is via the self-confidence that you are able to successfully detach from your ideas and perform by your values and standards.

Have you ever experienced low confidence previously? Are you still dealing with low confidence? If yes, then there is a high possibility that you currently have actually experienced rumination lots of times. Rumination just describes the propensity to replay worries and perceived missteps repeatedly.

When rumination is happening too often, this is connected to anxiety and, even in severe instances, depression. This is a thing which could induce you to disengage from the whole world around you.

Nevertheless, when you load your tank with self-confidence, there is significant energy that derives from inside you and works by breaking the cycle of negative attitude to ensure that your inner critic is quiet.

How to Be More Motivated

Building self-confidence is not a thing which you can accomplish just like that. It is a constant procedure which requires a great deal of little actions that leave a powerful feeling of enduring achievement. Well, it is more like discovering a new language, or being on a weight reduction regimen, or perhaps conquering a challenge. Think about it as a mastering a brand-new skill.

Well, you might be questioning what your grades or success with weight loss have to do with being self-confident. Something that you are going to discover is that those accomplishments you have had did not occur overnight. They must have taken some time and a great deal of determination. In case you are able to triumph through difficult circumstances and hardships, then you absolutely can replicate the identical grit and persistence in other parts of your life.

As your confidence continues to increase gradually, you are going to discover that your self-drive has strengthened, and your capabilities end up being deeply rooted and remarkable.

The voices that tell you that you might not make it are going to be silenced by the large smile on your face stating what if I make it! When you begin to see improvement, you are going to feel invigorated.

Be More Resilient

When you are confident, you are well geared up to deal with anything which occurs in your life. Even when confronted with extreme problems and failures, you just hold your head up, and shoulders back, and you give it one more shot. Believe me, even the most self-confident individuals on the planet fall short. So, this does not indicate that when you have confidence, you are never going to fail. It merely suggests that you are not going to remain down, beat yourself up, or end up being paralyzed by them. You are going to brace yourself and rise to the occasion of offering it another go.

Self-confidence is going to enable you to force yourself to have a go at brand-new methods, techniques, and ways to turn your dreams into reality. Simply put, when you fail or slip up, you are going to find out that they are a part of learning. Just through mistakes can we become a more powerful version of ourselves. It merely implies that you are going to accept failure, understanding that it is an aspect of life.

Studies have actually revealed that, paradoxically, when you don't mind failing, you are going to end up being more effective. The primary reason behind this is that you are not anticipating that everything is going to be completely flawless. When you take more shots, you could just improve.

Work on Your Relationships

This might sound a bit odd. Nevertheless, something that I have actually found out throughout the years is that the more self-confidence you cultivate, the less self-indulgent you end up being. Picture yourself strolling into a room filled with individuals when everybody is focusing on the speaker, and after that, there you come in to sit.

Many times, you are going to feel uncomfortable and assume that individuals are looking at you. Well, 90% of the time, folks are going to simply take a glimpse and pay no attention to you later. They are all wrapped up in their thoughts and feelings or what the speaker is speaking about, and absolutely nothing taking place beyond their zone of focus matters whatsoever.

Self-confidence erases the idea that you have to make an enduring impression on individuals, and you find yourself having fun with the crowd and taking pleasure in each part of your interaction. You are not going to be caught up in attempting to contrast yourself with other people. You just sink into an unwinded state which places everybody else at ease and thus assisting you to connect much deeper.

Studies have actually additionally revealed that having unstoppable self-confidence breeds compassion. The fact is, when you are less self-assured, all your thoughts are wandering around thinking about what individuals may be thinking. Nevertheless, when you are self-assured, you are comfy in your genuine identity, and your mind is in the present. Rather than allowing the outer environment impact your inner dialogue, you draw the attention somewhere else and concentrate on things which really matter at the moment. Put simply, you do not get consumed with insecurity. You reach out and elevate others.

Why Authenticity is so Powerful

It is just through self-confidence that you could go towards your complete potential. This is when you quickly embrace your weak points and failures with the understanding that these drawbacks do not alter your genuine feeling of self-regard. Rather, you value the truth that you have strengths you could honor even amidst all hardships and, thus, are empowered to utilize them totally.

To put it simply, strong self-confidence is what assists in lining up your actions with your values, fundamentals, and standards. This, consequently, provides you with a remarkable feeling of purpose. Self-confidence opens you up to self-discovery to ensure that you can value who you genuinely are and what you represent. When you see something which is wrong, you have the guts to appear, stand up, and be vocal over the concern. You easily enable your finest self to shine through.

Chapter 3: The Secret Code of Truly Confident Individuals

Here are the 3 most effective tricks of Truly Confident Individuals:

They Know How to Control Their Mind

Individuals who have sturdy self-confidence understand how to handle their minds at each instant. The reason you feel excessively nervous about that job interview or performance or presentation is due to the fact that you can't handle your state of mind well enough.

The great thing about our attitude is that we can quickly pick to change it at any time towards the direction we pick. Let us think about an instance where you are unwinding in your house on Saturday morning, enjoying breakfast with your family members. Unexpectedly, the phone rings. Suddenly, you were informed that you need to go to an immediate meeting in an hour! And you need to leave your family for this unforeseen meeting.

Wow! Anybody in their proper mind is going to feel surprised, upset, and nervous being placed in such a circumstance. Nevertheless, all you need to do is attempt to quickly move your focus from delighting in family time to entering the confident, top-level meeting attitude.

Nobody claimed that this would be simple, due to the fact that it is not. However, the initial thing you ought to do is attempt and gain information from your manager regarding the meeting expectations, the program, the stakeholders sitting in the meeting, and other essential details. You might then speak with your loved ones about what just took place and get started.

Something that is necessary to note is that when a brand-new, unanticipated circumstance emerges, you need to accept that you are going to feel annoyed, challenged and stressed. Nevertheless, you could trick your brain into the appropriate mindset and get the crucial things done immediately. Initially, this might not be simple. Nevertheless, as you acquire more understanding and learn from experience, you are going to be psychologically ready for unforeseen occasions such as these constantly.

Merely ask yourself whether there is something whatsoever that is going to get you in the appropriate mindset. Think about your brain like Google. Anything you ask is going to be responded to.

They Have a Dream

If you want confidence, the secret is having a sense of direction in which your life is heading. Simply a straightforward question like, "What would you like your life to be like?" suffices to aid you to place things into perspective. Identify what the life of your dreams is like and how to measure your level of success. Then compose all your answers on a piece of paper.

Preferably, you ought to rise every morning and read what is on that paper about the life of your dreams and take a couple of minutes to imagine it. As days pass, you could include aditional specifics to the life of your dreams. By beginning the day like that, you really impress rock-solid self-confidence into your subconsciousness. This is going to additionally tell you what actions you need to take to bring you nearer to the life of your dreams.

They Aren't Worried About What Other People Think About Them

In the event that you want rock-solid self-confidence, you need to come to terms with the reality that individuals are going to judge constantly. This indicates that the only individual that you truly ought to be impressing is you! Unstoppable self-confidence originates from establishing your expectations and, after that, giving your all to hit them. There is absolutely nothing which you stand to acquire when you compare your objectives with other individuals' expectations.

Well, do not get me wrong, healthy competition isn't bad! When you have terrific motivators in life, you are going to strive to work hard and model their successes constantly. In the event that you are an athlete, imagine yourself smashing your personal all-time best record. Despite the fact that you may have come in 2nd in a race, you ought to not be dissatisfied due to the fact that you have actually done your finest and shattered your own record. That is all that is truly important.

Each and every single day, actively do the appropriate thing and offer it your finest, and after that, proceed and take pride in the individual you are. In the event that you have a powerful wish to leave your job and create your own business in pursuit of your dreams, then, indeed, make it happen! It matters not what individuals think. All that is important is that you are in a race for the supreme reward- the life of your dreams!

That being state, having sturdy self-confidence is not an effortless endeavor. You need to discover how to lock out all the outer noise to make sure that you are able to hear your inner voice. In the event that you constantly live your life pleasing others, you are never ever going to pursue your dreams confidently. A life of remorse is a life which we ought to constantly keep away from. Unstoppable self-confidence comes when you quit being managed by individuals and rather take control of your own life and drive it in the direction you wish to go.

Chapter 4: How to Start Developing Confidence

Leave Your Comfort Zone

In case you are going to have unshakeable self-confidence, you need to want to get out of your comfort zone to ensure that you could do stuff out of the norm. You need to incite that desire burning inside you to be remarkable.

Maybe you have a dazzling idea which you think might help your company, yet you do not know how to discuss that with your boss. Maybe you have a crush which you never tried to talk to.

The issue which arises with not acting upon these wishes is that you are going to stagnate right where you are. Reality is, when you fall short to explore brand-new experiences, you are allowing fear remove your sunlight. You are just going deeper into your comfort zone. The hole which you have been sitting in for numerous years now.

Yes, it might be daunting to make the initial approach, running the risk of being humiliated by failures. However, in case you considering it, it's only 'FEAR'-- False Evidence Appearing Real. What is the worst that could occur? Frequently, you are simply overthinking. Getting out of your comfort zone could be so complicated, however, it is essential in case you want to fulfill your life's purpose and have unstoppable self-confidence. This might be how you can lastly demonstrate to yourself that you are able to accomplish whatever you set your mind to.

Besides, what is the worst thing which could take place? You could share your idea with your boss and guide the business to success, or the boss merely turns it down. You might ask that boy or girl out, and they might say either yes or no -- You additionally get your response without squandering a lot of time presuming. In any case, it is a win-win scenario.

Having self-confidence begins with you!

Something that I am going to tell you, without a doubt, is that to leave your comfort zone, you need to begin setting micro-goals which are going to all ultimately amount to the larger picture. Micro-goals merely describe little pieces of the bigger goal you have. When you split your larger goals into pieces, achieving them ends up being rather simple, and you are going to have a lot of fun while you're at it. This is going to additionally develop your momentum to keep pressing up until you have actually hit your goal.

Let us return to the instance we just discussed previously. So, you have a business idea or approach which you want to share with your boss, yet you don't feel you have the guts to do it. What you may do rather is break your major outcome into tinier goals that ultimately yield comparable results. Take little actions to get going, regardless of how little it is. Rather than taking the huge leap and feeling swamped, beginning small is going to take the pressure off you. When you carry this out, you make things rather easy to deal with, and you make follow-ups effortless.

So you like that boy or girl and have no guts to tell them that. However, she or he might not be single, to begin with. Your micro goal ought to be to create a rapport with them initially before you dive into the inmost end of things. Even prior to asking them out on a date, get to know who they are by simply starting a brief chat with him/her. Isn't that much better? This does not seem as if you are a stalker.

That state, you need to value that as you establish micro-goals, it enables you to get out of your comfort zone. As you accomplish your micro-goals one by one, you are going to understand that each little win can assist you in getting the self-confidence you require to progress. Challenge yourself that you will do something off the beaten track daily and see how that improves your self-confidence.

Know that You Are Valuable

Did you know that individuals with unstoppable self-confidence are frequently really resolute? Something which is quite exceptional with effective individuals is that they do not take too much time attempting to make little decisions. They merely do not overanalyze things. The reason why they are able to make quick decisions is since they currently understand their big picture, the utmost outcome.

How can you specify what you desire?

The initial step is to specify your values. Based upon Tony Robbins, an author, there are 2 primary values; means values and end values. These 2 kinds of values are connected to the emotions you want; joy, feeling of security, and satisfaction, to name a few.

Means Values

These just describe manners in which you can activate the emotion you want. An excellent instance is cash, which typically functions as a mean, not an end. It is something that is going to provide you financial flexibility, something which you desire, and that is why it is a means value.

Ends Values

This describes emotions which you are searching for, such as love, joy, and a feeling of security. They are just the important things that your means values provide. For example, cash is going to provide you with stability and financial security.

To put it simply, the means values are the things that you believe you want for you to obtain the end values. The most essential thing is for you to have understanding of what you value to make sure that you could make educated decisions a lot quicker. This, consequently, is going to provide you with a solid feeling of identity, which is where you draw long-lasting self-confidence from. You need to be in control of your life and not vice versa.

One way you may do that is by making sure that you specify your end values. You could begin by committing at least an hour or two weekly to jot down what are your end values. To arrive there, begin by mentioning what your values are that you wish to refine to reach your dream life.

A few of the questions which may aid you to place things into perspective consist of:

- What are a couple of things which are important to you?

- Are there things in your life which you do not care about?

- In case you were to make a hard decision, what are a few of the values which you are going to stand by and what are those which you are going to disregard?

- In case you have or had children, what are some of the values you are going to impart in them?

Accept Change

Were you ever in a situation where you are stressing about the past or the future? This is one thing that a lot of us end up doing. Nevertheless, here is the important thing; the individual you were 5 years ago or are going to be 5 years from now is really not the same person you are currently.

You are going to discover that 5 years back, your taste, interests, and buddies are not the same as they are today and odds are that they are going to be different 5 years in the future. The point is, it is vital that you accept who you are today and understand that you are evolving all the time.

Based on research carried out by Carol Dweck, it is apparent that kids succeed at school once they embrace a growth mindset. Actually, with the growth mindset, they trust that they can be successful in a specific topic. This is the reverse of what kids with a fixed mindset experience due to the fact that they think that they can't change or influence what was given to them. For that reason, having the idea that you can not expand just restricts your self-confidence.

You need to stop judging yourself in order to accept all that you are. The majority of the time, we are out there judging individuals by what they say, the way in which they say it, their clothes, and their behavior. Similarly, we judge ourselves in our minds contrasting our previous and current self.

For you to establish a solid sense of self-confidence, it is essential that you begin by surpassing the routine of self-judgment and adverse criticism. Indeed, this is a thing which could be challenging in the beginning, however, when you begin to practice it, you understand how backward that was.

You could begin by selecting at least a couple of days weekly when you stay away from making any judgment whatsoever. If you have got absolutely nothing positive to say, do not say it. In case there is a harmful thought which crosses the mind, you substitute it with a beneficial one. Slowly, your mind is going to begin priming to a state of non-judgment, and it is going to end up being your normal state of mind quickly. This is not going to just assist with accepting others yet additionally with embracing yourself for who you genuinely are.

Be in The Moment

Sounds easy, right? This is vital and essential for you to develop your self-confidence. By being in the moment, you are basically enabling your body, mind, and soul to be involved in the activity at hand.

Let us picture talking to somebody who is not listening to what you have to say. This is one thing which a lot of us have likely experienced. How did you feel? Meanwhile, imagine talking to somebody, and you feel like you were the only individual in the room. Feels quite special, huh?

That person was present at the moment, and that's why you felt special. They paid extremely close attention to what you were saying, feeling every feeling with you. They were involved in the exchange at a much deeper level. By doing this, you can hold on to information while still experiencing compassion.

To be present, you need to cultivate a psychological double-check. This merely implies that you ought to psychologically check-in on yourself routinely. To do that, you need to establish a psychological trigger or calendar by asking yourself where your mind is. When you do this, you are just observing your mind.

Are you thinking about supper reservations during a meeting? Do you believe that you are not enough? To gain control of these negative thoughts, you have to check in on yourself from time to time psychologically. As soon as you have the response to your question, breathe in deeply and return your focus on your essential things.

Chapter 5: How to Stand up for Yourself

Many people do not know how to stand up for themselves when needed. There are individuals out there who are going to constantly be expecting your downfall and squashing your self-confidence, in case, you do not understand how to stand up for what yourself. In case you wish to live a life with unstoppable self-confidence, begin by finding out how to stand up for yourself.

Know What You Want

This is the initial step; understanding what you desire. When individuals come charging at you from all directions, what do you want as the end result? Do you want them to stop being ill-mannered? When you understand what you want out of a scenario or what goals you have, you are going to have the power to manage the scenario without letting the scenario to get out of control.

Understand the Truth Behind Your Responses

Something that you need to keep in mind here is that how you react originates from your own experience, filter and you want to comprehend the truth that others can have an opinion that is different from yours. If you put in the time to comprehend that reality, you are going to understand that you can't constantly change others. Changing how you see things from inside is the only thing you can change. Simply acknowledging that is going to set you free from constantly feeling daunted by other individuals's behavior.

Nonetheless, you never want to get to the point where you are desperate for somebody else's approval. It is about you guaranteeing that before you can deal with anybody, you plainly understand what your values are and that you won't compromise your integrity.

Let go of Attachment

We have actually discussed earlier that it is necessary that you understand what you are after and how you view other individuals' expectations. Additionally, you need to comprehend that you can not expect another person to change just because that is what you want.

For that reason, instead of wagering your joy on others, merely accept that behaviors are difficult to alter and relinquish any attachment. It is natural for everybody to wish for an unhealthy scenario to change. Nevertheless, wagering your joy on their change is a losing game.

Put it on Paper Before You Do Anything

This is pretty straightforward. There are a lot of things which individuals are going to do or say that are going to make you mad. Nevertheless, what genuinely matters is guaranteeing that you do not let that anger become an attack.

Create Some Time To Have A Talk

Well, there is constantly that wish to place somebody in their deserved place, something which works completely well in films. Nevertheless, in real life, this does not come as a really useful approach. The best means through which you can create a change in your relationship is through a real conversation. A proper talk is about having an adult conversation instead of merely talking down upon people.

Know When to Stop Talking

This is most likely a thing which lots of folks see as an indication of weakness. Well, in this particular case, understanding when to stop talking is a kind of confidence. It is an indication that you understand your values and do not let others determine who you are. You understand what your actual identity is, and you do not feel the requirement to prove yourself to other folks and plead for validation.

Instead of losing your energy and time attempting to engage with individuals who are plainly stubborn with how they see things, the largest favor you may do for yourself is just to walk away. This is a step that just genuinely confident folks do due to the fact that they understand what is vital to them, what they desire, and they value their time.

With self-confidence, you understand that your time is far too valuable to squander on individuals who have no regard for others and themselves. In case some people can not appreciate individuals around them, then you understand that they are not the sort of folks you wish to squander your time on.

In case you attempt to take them down, you are not going to feel any better. You need to comprehend that standing up for yourself does not constantly imply that you need to win. Merely leave so that you make more time and space for individuals that are going to accept, embrace, and honor you as you are. This is the supreme road of those with unstoppable self-confidence.

Chapter 6: How to Keep Going After Failure

Accept Failure

Although failure is genuinely uncomfortable, you need to comprehend that it is a chance to learn. When you are attempting to make something, you have to accept the truth that things are never going to be ideal, which is why failures are bound to occur every now and then.

From each failure, ask yourself what can you gain from it, and what are you going to do in a different way following time. This is going to make sure that you can carry out correct methods in your next undertaking to make sure that these things do not take place again. Among the best lessons you can gain is how to fail with dignity. By doing this, you get to find out the needed lessons to improve your ingenuity.

Give Your People an Opportunity to Fail

It is not only a select few who fail. Everybody is going to mess something up in a company. If you aim to be a prosperous leader, then you ought to discover how to assume responsibility for your people, regardless of how long they have been there.

Let your workers be responsible for their actions and offer them time to correct their errors. When you lead individuals through failure, your attention ought to be on ensuring that they gained something from their mistakes and failed forward. In case they fail to learn from previous mistakes and redo them repeatedly, you can then think about letting them go.

Promptly Apologize When Necessary

When you deal with an issue, it is essential that you promptly fix it. The worst thing you may do when an issue emerges is neglecting them or sweeping problems beneath the rug. If you do this in a business, the odds are that your customers are going to lose trust in you and leave. The ideal strategy is to say you're sorry and proceed.

Look at Your Failures

In case there is anybody that needs to deal with missteps and failures, it is you. In case you are the one behind the mess, then you ought to be prepared to deal with it. Simply do your finest to maintain the damage under wraps. In case there is collateral damage at the same time, the ideal thing to do is apologize as quickly as you are able to in order to bring back the trust.

Carry On

Life happens in spite of failures. Whenever you fall, it is essential that you do not remain down but instead pick yourself up and keep going. The trick is for you to make an effort repeatedly up until you attain your objectives. With each failure, there is a lesson, and the better you end up being in dealing with the identical circumstance. With more skills, you have more self-confidence. Whatever takes place, simply bear in mind that what is necessary is to maintain your eyes on the utmost prize.

Did you understand that being consumed by failures shuts off the brain's inspirational centers? This implies that you need to discover how to frame failures in manners in which make you feel inspired. If things are untenable, there is a high probability that the result is going to be an ineffective business endeavor. Failing is not the end of everything!

How to Achieve Micro-Goals

Put Them on Paper

Jotting down your goals guarantees that you analyze each little detail and how every activity is going to be realized to achieve the goal ultimately. It additionally guarantees that you can remember your targets due to the fact that research has actually revealed a powerful connection between memory retention and writing.

Specify the Goals

It is essential that you choose at least a certain time and day whenever you are going to commit to dealing with your micro goals. You could additionally set up a note on your phone to ensure that it can consistently condition you to ease into a routine of performing towards those targets.

Keep an Eye on Your Goals Routinely

It is essential that you track your goals routinely on a weekly or month-to-month basis. Each time you achieve any of these goals, your brain is going to be trained to concentrate on what matters most and begin attaining more!

See Your Goals in Your Mind

The other crucial idea is for you to visualize yourself having achieved the goals. Studies have actually shown that the motor portion of the brain is going to be turned on whenever you carry out the activities physically. One study had 2 groups; one that engaged in the piano playing physically and a different one that played piano psychologically.

The most fascinating thing was that people who practiced through visualization were equally as successful as those who physically practiced. This shows that you do not need to physically practice something to become proficient at that thing. This study clarifies the strength of visualization and you too ought to utilize visualization to improve at any skill or attain any goal.

Chapter 7: Actionable Tips & Exercises

Grow Your Knowledge

The initial step to cultivating your self-confidence is making sure that you acquire knowledge both in your private and professional undertakings. There is constantly that area for which you sense you are lacking in understanding and knowledge.

If you wish to have more self-confidence, then you need to show mastery in this field. You can broaden your understanding by attending online courses, participating in comparable conferences and occasions, along with reading books. The other thing which you could delight in while acquiring knowledge are teleclasses, where you get to communicate and participate in peer discussions. This is going to go a long way in enhancing your degree of self-confidence.

Appreciate Smaller Wins

Strong self-confidence originates from the capability to celebrate and experience little successes and victories. Consider this as providing prizes for using knowledge. Do you remember the part about micro-goals? Well, every time you attain a micro-goal, you award yourself. Yes, they are not the supreme goal, yet they are little pieces which comprise the larger goal.

The prize does not need to be large. Even a basic pat on the back or simply a straightforward compliment from an associate is enough to improve your amount of self-confidence. For that reason, make sure that you monitor each little accomplishment and enable yourself to experience it totally. By doing this, you are going to begin to feel your self-confidence growing each and every single day.

Believe in Something

Among the qualities I appreciate about confident individuals is that they believe in a supreme being. They think that the maker of the universe has a role for each living soul. Simply put, the reason why we are on the planet right now is to find and fulfill our larger purpose.

Simply put, they appear to have superb knowledge that when they follow the plan of the creator, attaining success is simply a question of time. For that reason, if you really wish to accomplish success, you need to have faith that it is achievable. It is essential that you have undeviating faith in your ability. When your faith is loaded with enthusiasm, then there is a high probability that you are going to follow your real purpose.

Cultivate A Firm Resolve

Within this life, it is natural that you are going to deal with obstacles and frustrations in the process. It is, for that reason, natural to feel mad and dissuaded. Nevertheless, it is essential that you see these problems as a chance for learning for something larger yet to take place in your future.

When you show faith in your capabilities, you are going to surpass discouragements and get a strong resolve. It is this resolve which is going to, consequently, help you conquer challenges. This is primarily since strong resolve is a real mark of perseverance at work. Instead of despairing, you are going to understand that without these difficulties, you would not have a growth mindset. It is vital that your mind is concentrated on the desired result and not on obstructions. Rather than thinking about a thousand reasons why you can't, think about one reason why you can.

With time, you are going to see your talents turn into skills. It is just then that you are going to start to see what is genuinely feasible, a measure of success guiding you forward with a lot of vitality and passion. It is this passion which is going to keep you ignited to keep scoring those little micro-goals.

Work With Professionals

Determine places where you have gaps in understanding which you wish to fill up. As soon as you do that, get assistance from experts that are going to assist you in acquiring more experience and knowledge. Understanding that you have professionals' assistance, you are going to additionally be more confident when acting and deciding. You can learn from professionals from books, videos, blogs, one-on-one meetings, phone calls, workshops, and so on. The benefit of an expert coach is that they are going to assist you to stay accountable for each action you take in finishing your program.

Keep in mind that, if you desire self-confidence, then you need to draw in self-confidence. Yes, professionals are going to show you the way, however, they are not going to walk the road for you. You need to want to go through all challenges with your head held high your eyes on the reward. Ultimately, you are going to arrive there.

Visualize Your Confident Self

When you are able to view yourself as somebody confident, then self-confidence is going to end up being a characteristic which is simple and natural to demonstrate in reality. You begin to experience it directly. Take a moment to envision yourself having the self-confidence which you require in a particular scenario.

Picture how you would think and behave if you had the self-confidence you are after. Preferably, shut your eyes and see yourself utilizing your mind's eye, acting with a lot of self-conviction and confidence. Maintain that image in your mind, and you are going to understand that your vision is going to start taking root and coming true.

Believe That You Deserve Confidence

Did you understand that expectations are faith at work? At this moment, you have currently imagined yourself being self-assured and how you would feel after that. When you are self-confident, you are going to speak, act, and move surely and with a lot of passion as you go after your objectives. This is when you understand that you have the emotions, sight, and actions of a self-confident individual. Simply put, you are going to be far better positioned to accomplish a lot more than you expected. When you anticipate to be confident, it comes to fruition.

Like we have actually currently stated, self-confidence is not a thing which occurs over night. You need to put these actionable suggestions into practice over the course of months. Begin by jotting down methods in which you plan to use these actions. In this manner, you understand precisely how it would be like to act towards your goal. When you act upon them, you begin understanding significant improvements in your self-confidence, and quickly this equates to self-confidence, joy, happiness, and supreme success.

Chapter 8: Importance of Buddies

You might be wondering, what do buddies have to do with confidence? Every one of us has times of insecurity and self-doubt. It is extremely common to be distressed about our appearance. Frequently, you might find yourself questioning whether you said the appropriate thing or did the appropriate thing in any presented circumstance. In some cases, it is anything as small as matching your dress with the appropriate set of shoes, or your t-shirt with the appropriate tie.

Similar to any other individual, when I am not exactly certain of these things, I rely on my buddies for the second point of view. Something that you might have seen is that specific individuals play an essential part in constructing our self-confidence. It is through buddies that we can shake the suspicion or skepticism we have about ourselves. Thanks to them you can make better decisions in your life.

These are a few of how reconnecting with buddies assists with developing self-confidence:

They Want You to Be Successful

If there is somebody who you contact when you have great news to share, it is your buddy. Buddies are individuals we could turn to when we have issues, disappointments, or problems. The primary reason is that they take pleasure in what we achieve. They are individuals who support us and trust that we are able to make it happen! Understanding that somebody's got your back is going to aid you to deal with anything with a lot of self-confidence.

They Are Good Models

No person is flawless, so the phrase goes. Nevertheless, with buddies, they additionally have strengths and capabilities which aid them to carry out better in what they do. I have a buddy who moves the crowd with his speech. At some time, I questioned whether I may do the identical. With someone to admire, it ended up being far easier to move towards my objective. By merely modeling his way of delivering speeches, I got better ultimately. The identical thing goes for you; having a buddy assists us to see how we could utilize their strengths to enhance our weak points.

They Support The Growth

Did you realize that in some cases, the one thing which is between your success and you is your attitude? Well, you do now. The reason you are hesitant about pursuing that business idea is that your mind is working against you. Nevertheless, when you are surrounded by good buddies, they are able to see strengths in you that you never ever realized were there. That is going to provide you with sufficient inspiration to keep going, and you will recognize that you simply required a small push to fly like an eagle.

They Make It Easier to Keep Going

Within this journey referred to as life, there are going to be bumps along the path constantly. It could be failing an exam, losing a competition, being dumped or perhaps worse, death a loved one. Nevertheless, when you have buddies, you have somebody to rely on when you're down. They are going to be there to provide you with insights from various points of view. They are going to bring a lot of light to your darkest times.

They Show Us the Power of Teamwork

Self-confidence is not only working alone. It is about understanding how to go alone when necessary and when to walk with a group. Often, when you are on your own, you might feel shy and unsure about heading to locations or trying brand-new things or doing things in a different way. Nevertheless, in case you are doing those things with a buddy, there is an unexpected burst of energy, and you start noticing lots of opportunities for creativity.

The reality is, the ideal aspect of reconnecting with buddies is the truth that feelings are mutual. They are individuals who share our dreams, and we should do the identical for them. So, surround yourself with genuine buddies and see how that affects your mindset and self-confidence to expand beyond what you thought was possible.

Conclusion

Undoubtedly, it is through self-confidence that we are able to obtain success and joy in life. Nevertheless, the most essential question you need to ask yourself is, how do you cultivate that self-confidence?

It is necessary for you to comprehend that self-confidence starts with your attitude. This is what is going to assist you in staying authentic and real to yourself. It is the thing which assists you to retain your real identity regardless of what situations you deal with in life. It aids to think about self-confidence as that person which ebbs and flows from you. With the clear steps that we have actually gone over within this guide, you are going to have the ability to develop self-confidence which lasts.

The secret is for you to be ready to set your mind towards attaining it. Then go and get out of your comfort zone, determine your values, and accept change by being in the moment. In this manner, you are going to have the fundamental self-confidence, and you are going to additionally motivate other people to become better.

I hope that you enjoyed reading through this book and that you have found it useful. If you want to share your thoughts on this book, you can do so by leaving a review on the Amazon page. Have a great rest of the day.

Printed in Great Britain
by Amazon